ISBN 0 361 05436 X
Copyright © 1982 Papal Visit Limited
Published 1982 by Purnell Books, Paulton, Bristol BS18 5LQ
Made and printed in Great Britain by Purnell and Sons
(Book Production) Limited, Paulton, Bristol BS18 5LQ

Colour reproduction by K.L.W. Plates Ltd., London

Acknowledgements

The publishers would like to thank the following for the use
of their photographs: 4, 5, 11 Camera Press; 6 John
Topham. All other photographs were researched at the
Pontificia Fotografia in Rome.

WESTMINSTER COUNCIL
OF CENSORSHIP

Title POPE JOHN PAUL II
 HIS STORY FOR CHILDREN

Author Brenda Ralph Lewis

Nihil obstat ANTON COWAN
 Censor

Imprimatur RT REV PHILIP HARVEY VG, OBE
 BISHOP IN NORTH LONDON

Westminster, 25TH MARCH 1982

The Nihil obstat *and* Imprimatur *are a declaration that a book or pamphlet
is considered to be free from doctrinal or moral error. It is not implied
that those who have granted the* Nihil obstat *and* Imprimatur *agree with the
contents, opinions or statements expressed.*

POPE JOHN PAUL II
His Story for Children

Brenda Ralph Lewis

Purnell

POPE JOHN PAUL II BRITISH VISIT 1982

ope John Paul II is many men to many people. To the world's 700 million Roman Catholics, he is the Holy Father, the leader of their faith, and the one to whom they look for guidance and advice. To the people of Poland, John Paul's native land, he is also a champion of human rights who brings them hope that their freedoms as human beings will not be crushed by the often harsh Communist government of their country. To everyone, whether Catholic or no, he is the man who speaks out strongly against those who cause the troubles and tragedies of the world — racial hatred, religious persecution, poverty, oppression or the plight of homeless refugees.

Pope John Paul is, therefore, a leader of world-wide importance, and through television, the newspapers and their reports about his extensive travels, he is also a celebrity.

Popes were not always celebrities. Far from it. In the past, people might know what they looked like, from photographs or paintings, but they never saw them in person or heard their voices except on a few important occasions. For until John Paul's predecessor, Paul VI, visited the Holy Land and India in 1964, the year after he was elected Pope, no Pope had ever journeyed outside Italy: instead, Popes remained mostly in the Vatican, the separate state within the capital of Italy, Rome, which is the home and headquarters of the Papacy.

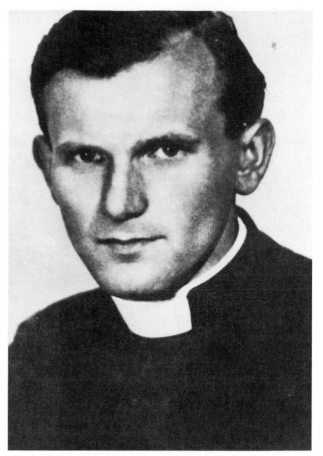

Far left **A photograph taken while the future Pope was still in primary school. Karol Wojtyla is on the left of the top row.**

Left **At the age of 12.**

Above **At the age of 26 in 1946.**

John Paul II has carried on where Pope Paul left off, and his visit to Britain between 28th May and 2nd June 1982 is only the latest in a long chronicle of travel. In 1979, only three months after his election as Pope, John Paul visited Mexico and the Dominican Republic in Central America, and afterwards went on to Poland, Ireland, the United States and Turkey. In 1980, he went to six countries in Africa, to Germany, Brazil and across the globe in the Far East, to the Philippine Islands, Guam and Japan. In February 1982, he went back to Africa, again visiting several countries there.

The vast extent of the Pope's travels shows, of course, how very far flung the Roman Catholic faith has become since Christianity was first established in Rome nearly 2,000 years ago. At that time, and for some time afterwards, Rome was the centre of the mightiest and most powerful state in Europe: the Roman Empire. The first Pope, St Peter, had been the chief Apostle of Jesus, and he died in Rome some time after the year 64 AD, during the persecution of the Christians by the Roman Emperor Nero. The persecution continued for a long time, but in 313 AD Christianity captured its most mighty convert: Emperor Constantine himself became a Christian, and the whole Empire with him.

When the Roman Empire disintegrated after about 476 AD, the Christian Church was the only organisation which could take over its power and influence in Europe. The process took a long time, and many missionaries risked many dangers and long, hard journeys to spread the Christian faith. The centre of this great missionary operation was Rome and, today, Catholics still regard the city and the Pope in the Vatican as the central edifice of their religion. The Pope, in fact, has many titles: he is Bishop of Rome, Supreme Pastor of the Universal Church, and is also called the Supreme Pontiff. The Pope is said to 'occupy the Chair' or 'Throne of St Peter' and to hold 'St Peter's Keys'. This is why two crossed keys, the papal symbol, appear in the centre of the special design for Pope John Paul's visit to Britain.

Right **A casual photograph taken on a country bicycling trip in the mountains of the Polish-Czech border.**
Far right **As a cardinal, Karol Wojtyla is seen here with Pope Paul VI.**

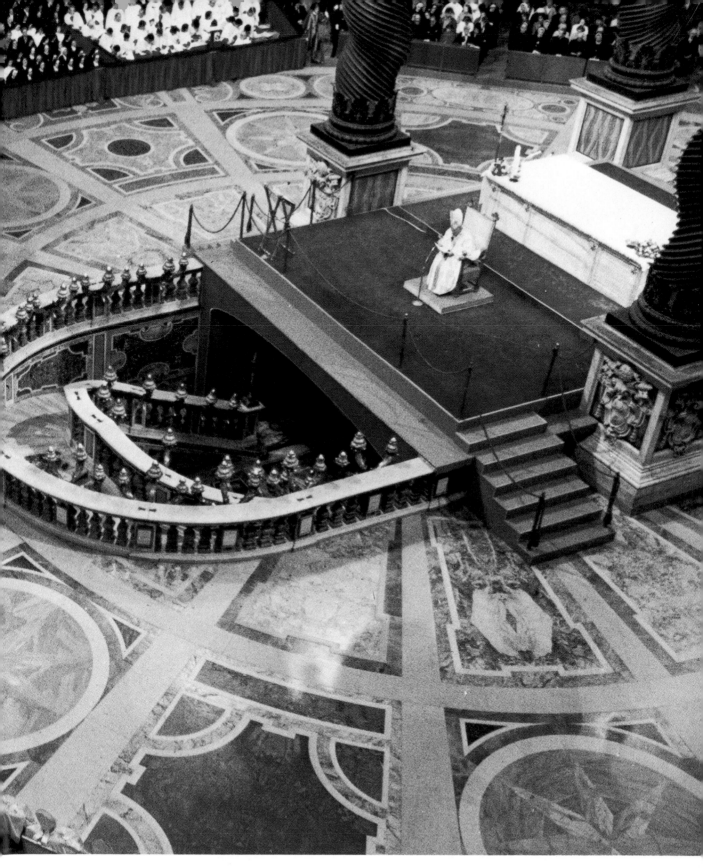

A view from above of the interior of St Peter's in Rome as Pope John Paul II conducts a service.

Pope John Paul II is the 263rd pontiff after St Peter, and he was elected from among the cardinals of the Roman Catholic Church in a remarkable, though rather sad year: 1978, since called 'The Year of the Three Popes'. On 6th August 1978, Pope Paul VI died after a reign of 15 years. His successor, chosen at the conclave, a secret meeting of cardinals, on 26th August, was Albino Luciani, Patriarch of Venice. The new Pope took the name John Paul I in honour of his two predecessors, Paul VI and, before him, Pope John XXIII. The first John Paul, unfortunately, reigned only a few weeks, for on 28th September, 33 days after his election, he was found dead in bed. The shock was very great, and so was the sadness, for despite the short time the world had known him, he had made a great impression with his charming smile and the humility which made him refuse the usual grand papal coronation.

This was unusual, but the cardinals' next choice, at a second conclave, on 16th October 1978, was even more so. When he was elected that day, the Cardinal Archbishop of Krakow, Karol Wojtyla — the real name of John Paul II — was the first Pole to become Pope, and at the age of 58 years, the youngest for over a hundred years. In addition, all Popes in the previous 460 years had been of Italian nationality, and very few, if any at all, had led early lives so full of danger and adventure as John Paul II.

When Karol Wojtyla was 19, in September 1939, his native Poland was overrun and occupied by the armies of neighbouring Nazi Germany. Two days later, on 3rd September, Britain and France, Poland's allies, declared war on Germany and the Second World War began. Karol Wojtyla, however, already knew what the war was going to be like. On Friday, 1st September when the invasion of Poland began, the town of Krakow, 50 km from Wadowice, where he was born on 18th May 1920, was bombed from the air by the Luftwaffe, the German airforce. That day, Karol braved the rain of bombs, the fires and the explosions to attend Mass, as usual, at Krakow Cathedral.

Every Sunday when he is in Rome, the Pope goes out on to the balcony outside his apartments to bless the crowds in St Peter's Square.

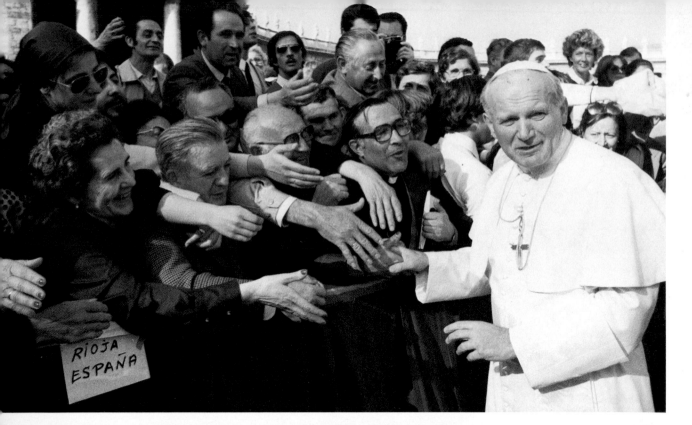

 **The Pope greeting the crowds in St Peter's Square.**

At this time, the future Pope was a student, but the occupying Nazis soon closed down all universities and other places of higher education. In order to earn a living, Karol went to work as a labourer in a stone quarry owned by a chemical works. Here, in conditions of freezing cold, he broke rocks with a sledgehammer and pushed barrowloads of stone to the nearby railway siding. Later, in the winter of 1941–42, Karol went to work in a water-purifying plant, carrying buckets of lime joined by a yoke across his neck.

In 1942, he began to study for the priesthood at a secret 'underground' seminary. He also joined the equally secret Rhapsody Theatre where he both acted in and produced plays. The Germans had made these activities

Pope John Paul meets people of all races and ages during his public audiences in Rome.

Above **The Pope greets a group of priests from the Philippines.**
Below and right **The Swiss Guards are the Pope's own personal bodyguard.**

Queen Elizabeth II of Great Britain and Prince Philip were welcomed by the Pope on their visit to Rome in October

1980. Lord Carrington, Foreign Secretary to Britain, is also seen here to the left of Prince Philip.

illegal and if the seminary or the theatre had been discovered, Karol and his friends would have been very severely punished.

There was, however, an even greater peril in another kind of secret undertaking in which Karol became involved: helping the Jews in Krakow to hide from the Germans who were determined to hunt them

Far left **Cardinal Hume, the Roman Catholic Primate of all England, on his visit to Rome early in 1982.**

Left **The Nigerian Ambassador to the Vatican presents his credentials to Pope John Paul II.**
Below **The Pope chats to some choir boys in St Peter's.**

down and kill them. Many times the future Pope risked death to smuggle Jewish families out of Krakow into the neighbouring small towns, or provide them with false identification papers so that the Germans would not discover who they were. Eventually, the name of Karol Wojtyla was put on the Nazis' 'black list' of wanted men.

In 1979 the Pope made a historic trip back to Poland, his native land. On his arrival he knelt and kissed the ground as he often does on his travels. Huge crowds turned out to greet him and welcome him home.

In these years, Karol came to know at first hand how much dreadful suffering there was in the world. Suffering, and terror, it seemed, was all around him. In August 1944, for instance, the Nazis began rounding up all men between the ages of 15 and 50 in Krakow. Sounds of shooting and violent struggle echoed through the streets as Karol knelt and prayed alone inside his house in Tyniecka Street: everyone else in the place had hidden away. By some miracle, however, the Nazis failed to search this particular house, and so Karol and the others survived. Millions, though, did not survive, but died horrific deaths in ghastly circumstances. Near

Krakow lay the notorious Auschwitz death camp where thousands of Jews, Poles, Russians and others were murdered by the Nazis. Karol Wojtyla never forgot these appalling crimes, and some forty years later, in 1979, when he returned to Poland as Pope, he visited the death camp at Birkenau, and went on to Auschwitz to say mass on the site of Auschwitz, where he prayed, and wept, for the four million people who had died there.

Pope John Paul conducted services and open-air masses all over Poland where thousands of people came to hear him and receive his blessing. He visited Warsaw (*right*), Krakow and Wadowice, his own home town, among many other places.

Right **A young boy scout receives the sacrament at an open-air mass in Galway.**

Far right **A solemn moment.**

The end of the Second World War, in 1945, did not mean the end of trouble and danger for Poland, or for Karol Wojtyla, who was ordained priest in Krakow on 1st November 1946. Poland was already well on the way to becoming a Communist state and in 1948, when the Communists at last seized power, they set about imprisoning anyone thought to be against their government. Communism was, and still is, an anti-religious creed, and one of the prisoners at this time was the Head of the Church in Poland, Cardinal Wyszynski.

Father Karol Wojtyla, now parish priest in the village of Niegowic near Krakow, seemed as unafraid of the Communists as he had been of the Germans during the War. He defied them by giving the children of Niegowic religious education and, dressed in ordinary everyday clothes, played football with them in the fields outside the village. Many other Polish priests were in prison for activities like this. In addition, Father Wojtyla wrote poetry for a Catholic newspaper in Krakow — of which the Communists did not approve. Later, he became professor of theology (religion) at the Polish State University, until the Communist government closed down the theology department.

Pope John Paul visits Knock in Southern Ireland, where a miracle is said to have occurred.

Even while he travels the Pope is constantly at work preparing for his next engagement, but, as usual, he finds the time to talk to and take an interest in the people around him.

By 1958, Karol Wojtyla, now aged 38 years, became Poland's youngest bishop, when he was appointed Bishop of Ombi. In 1964, he was made Archbishop of Krakow, and in 1967, a Cardinal. By this time, it became clear to many people, not only inside the Church, that Karol was outstanding in many ways. He was courageous, warm-hearted and compassionate. He lived very simply and humbly and worked extremely hard. There were times when he did not even bother to sleep, but worked on through the night. Yet he was also very approachable and always had time to meet people and talk over their problems with them. He was willing, too, to drop whatever he was doing and even get up in the middle of the night to visit the sick and dying.

When he had some well-deserved free time, Cardinal Archbishop Wojtyla, who was well built, athletic and had enormous physical energy, liked to indulge in all kinds of sports: canoeing, mountain-climbing,

Pope John Paul was warmly greeted by huge crowds all over the USA.

tennis, volleyball, swimming, skating, cross-country running, and, above all, skiing. He would ski down the slopes in the Tatra Mountains for hours on end and enjoyed to the full the thrill and danger of hurtling across the snow at top speed. He was, it appears, quite a daredevil. Though in his forties, Karol Wojtyla was so enthusiastic, energetic and fit that he was once taken for a much younger, much more junior man by an old parish priest who did not know him. This priest asked Karol to run errands for him, carry messages and do other humble tasks, and he did all he was asked without saying a word. Only later, by accident, did the old priest discover that his cheerful, willing 'errand boy' was a cardinal and an archbishop.

On his visit to the United Nations building in New York the Pope was met by Kurt Waldheim, General Secretary of the UN (*below*) and by children representing many nations around the world.

Above **Smiling from his car, the Pope acknowledges the crowds along the route of his motorcade.**
Left **The Pope is seen here on the balcony of the White House with President and Mrs Carter.**

Right **Beneath the statue of Christ the Redeemer in Rio de Janeiro, during the trip Pope John Paul made to Brazil in 1980.**

As a cardinal, Karol Wojtyla became a world-wide traveller, for he often went abroad to attend Church conferences and other important Church events. He went to Australia, the Far East, America and many countries in Western Europe. In 1973, Karol Wojtyla went to the Philippine Islands, where a prominent citizen, Jeremias Montemayor, expressed what many others felt about him. "As he grasps your hand," said Montemayor, "you immediately feel his great strength, not only of his body, but of his character. His eyes tell you of his big, pure heart. As he puts his arm around your shoulders, you feel his warm compassion, his deep sincerity, his fierce loyalty ..."

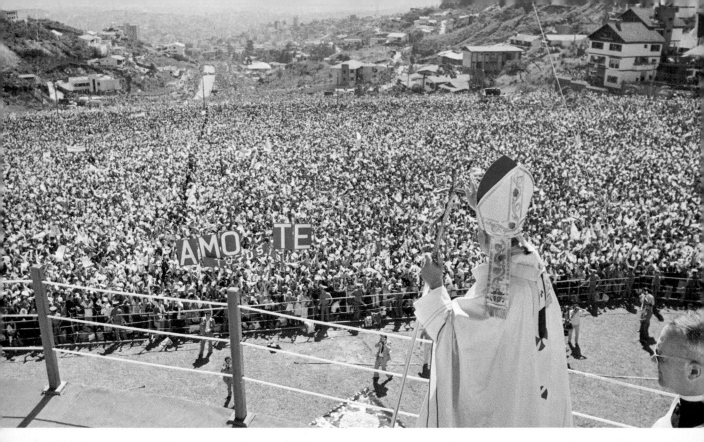

As always on his world trips, people came in their thousands to see and greet the Pope on his Brazilian visit.

In 1982 the Pope visited Japan. Here he is seen blessing some schoolchildren and also a young priest at his ordination.

Five years later, Jeremias Montemayor was among thousands of admirers of Karol Wojtyla who were not at all surprised when he was elected as Pope John Paul II. It was clear from the first what kind of Pope the second John Paul was going to be. What Montemayor called his 'warm compassion' made him break with tradition and leave the Vatican on the evening of his election to visit his old friend Bishop Andrea Deskur, who was in hospital after a heart attack: previously, Popes had not left the Vatican until they were inaugurated. The new Pope was also a man who had no time for or interest in material possessions or rich surroundings; he decided to follow the example of John Paul I in forgoing an elaborate coronation. Instead, John Paul II simply received the pallium, a white woollen scarf, circular in shape, with six crosses woven around the neck, which is the symbol of the office of Pope.

Since then, on his far-ranging journeys round the world, millions have been able to witness his 'big pure heart' when John Paul gives a special greeting to children, for whom he has particular affection, or when he bestows his blessing on vast crowds who come to greet him. The crowds are so huge that only very large open spaces can contain them. On 10th June 1979, when he celebrated mass on the last day of his tour of Poland, something like two million people were present. Some three months later, in Dublin, on the first day of his tour of Ireland, 1.2 million people came to see Pope John Paul celebrate Mass in Phoenix Park. On 3rd October, in New York, the Pope was given a traditional 'tickertape' welcome as he drove through Manhattan, and in Brazil, which he visited in the summer of 1980, he was seen by at least 20 million people and travelled some 19,000 miles.

On many of his public appearances, whether at home in Rome or abroad, Pope John Paul has gone among the crowds, sometimes on foot, sometimes by car, to talk face to face with ordinary people. Unfortunately, this wish to be close to people also puts the Pope in

Pope John Paul visited Africa in 1982. Here he is seen in Nigeria where excited crowds turned out to greet him wherever he went. Despite his busy programme, the Pope still found time to meet and talk to as many individual people as possible.

danger, like any other prominent public figure. This became clear on 13th May 1981 when the world was horrified to learn that a young Turkish terrorist, Mehmet Ali Agca, had shot and seriously wounded the Pope during a Public Audience in St Peter's Square, Rome. It took two surgical operations and a long convalescence before the Pope recovered, and the world breathed a great sigh of thankfulness and relief.

There was special relief in Britain, because it looked for a while as if the Pope would have to cancel his visit. When he arrives in London on Friday 28th May, he will, strictly speaking, be coming on a pastoral visit to Britain's Roman Catholic community. However, there is an additional purpose, for as the Pope himself has implied, the visit is a gesture of friendship to the British people as a whole. And as so many others have discovered in countries the world over, the friendship and concern of John Paul II, whose motto is 'Totus Tuus' — 'Totally Yours' — is something of great value and much pride.

Pope John Paul is especially fond of children and throughout his travels all over the world, he always finds the time to speak to and bless his young friends.